Timeline of Guy Fawkes

13 April 1570

Guy Fawkes is born in York, England, son of Edward Fawkes, a lawyer, and his wife, Edith.

1603

Fawkes travels to Spain and Italy to ask Catholic kings to invade England. They refuse.

1591

Fawkes leaves England to be a soldier in Europe.

1579

Fawkes's father (a Protestant) dies. A few years later, his mother marries a Catholic.

1604

Fawkes joins Catholic plotters led by Robert Catesby. They plan the Gunpowder Plot.

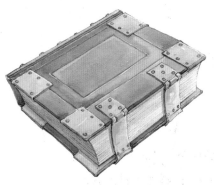

c.1585–1591

Fawkes works for Catholic nobles in Yorkshire.

9 November 1605

After torture in prison, Fawkes reveals details of the Gunpowder Plot.

May 1605

Fawkes travels to Europe again seeking support for the Gunpowder Plot.

31 January 1606

Fawkes falls from the scaffold and dies. His body is cut into pieces and put on public display, as a warning to future plotters.

4/5 November 1605

Gunpowder is found by royal guards. Fawkes is arrested.

June-July 1605

Fawkes, disguised as caretaker 'John Johnson', stores gunpowder in a cellar below the House of Lords.

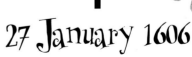

27 January 1606

Fawkes and the other plotters are put on trial, found guilty, and condemned to death.

Europe at war

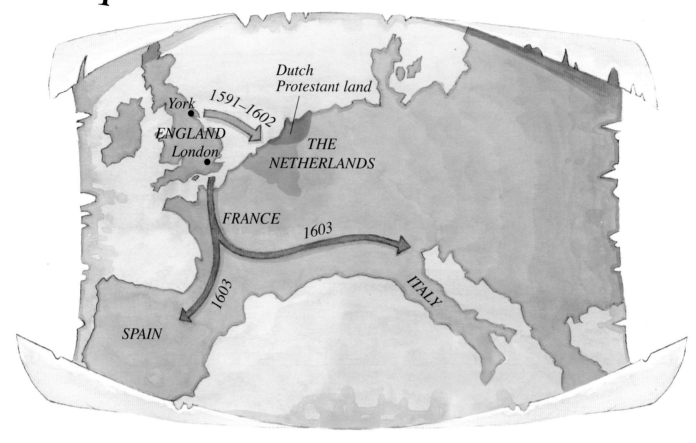

In Guy Fawkes's time, the Netherlands, Belgium and Luxembourg were ruled by Spain. The Spanish kings were Catholics, and supported Catholic rebels in many countries, including England. They also fought the rival Catholic rulers of France.

In 1581, Dutch Protestants who wanted independence took control of the northern Netherlands, starting a war with Spain that lasted until 1648. Catholic soldiers from all over Europe, including Guy Fawkes, joined the Spanish army to fight them, with pikes, muskets – and gunpowder!

Author:

Fiona Macdonald studied history at
Cambridge University, England, and at the
University of East Anglia. She has taught in
schools, adult education and universities, and is
the author of numerous books for children on
historical topics.

Artist:

David Antram was born in Brighton, England,
in 1958. He studied at Eastbourne College of Art
and then worked in advertising for 15 years before
becoming a full-time artist. He has illustrated many
children's non-fiction books.

Series creator:

David Salariya was born in Dundee, Scotland.
He has illustrated a wide range of books and
has created and designed many new series for
publishers in the UK and overseas. In 1989, he
established The Salariya Book Company.

Editor: **Jacqueline Ford**

Editorial Assistant: **Mark Williams**

Published in Great Britain in MMXVII by
Book House, an imprint of
The Salariya Book Company Ltd
25 Marlborough Place, Brighton BN1 1UB
www.salariya.com
www.book-house.co.uk

ISBN: 978-1-911242-41-3

S A L A R I Y A

1 3 5 7 9 8 6 4 2

A CIP catalogue record for this book is available
from the British Library.

Printed and bound in China.
Printed on paper from sustainable sources.

Visit
www.salariya.com
for our online catalogue and
fun **free** stuff.

PAPER FROM
SUSTAINABLE
FORESTS

You Wouldn't Want to Be Guy Fawkes!™

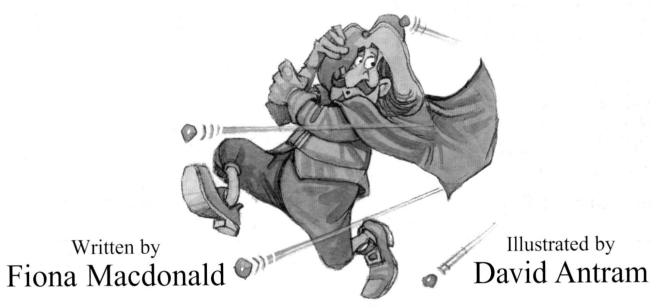

Written by
Fiona Macdonald

Illustrated by
David Antram

A Plot You'd Rather Not Know About

Created and designed by
David Salariya

BOOK HOUSE
a SALARIYA *imprint*

Contents

Introduction 9

Could you survive in troubled times? 10

Want to worship your own way? 12

Should you flee, and seek your fortune? 14

Will you welcome the new king? 16

Can you find friends who share your fears? 18

Do you really want to kill King James?! 20

Who will do the dreadful deed? 22

Can you keep the plot a secret? 24

Will you escape, and survive? 26

Could you survive terrible torture? 28

...then face a dreadful death? 30

Will they remember, remember...? 32

Glossary 34

Index 36

Introduction

The place? Tudor England. The year? Around 1590. You're a nine-year-old boy in Yorkshire, England, and already hard at work. You're a servant in a fine house belonging to the Bainbridge family. They are rich and powerful with close connections to the Lord Mayors of York. York is a big and busy city, and Yorkshire people are proud of their traditional way of life. Like many others in the north of England, they have their own independent ideas, and don't always approve of what is happening down south in London. That's England's capital and home to its famous Queen, Elizabeth I. You've never been there, but one day, you will… Read on, and find out more.

Could you survive in troubled times?

You live at a time when England has been made miserable by religious quarrels. Families have split, communities have shattered, and many people have died because of different ideas about the Christian religion. Some people love and respect old Catholic beliefs; others, called Protestants, think these are wrong and need reform. They dislike Catholic priests and prayers. They can't understand Latin, the language of the Catholic Church, and want to read the Bible in English. In Yorkshire, you meet people on both sides of the quarrel: Catholics and Protestants. They (and you) are angry, unhappy – and frightened.

The story so far..

ALL CHANGE! Protestant preachers throughout Europe call for religious reform. They win many followers – and make many enemies.

SMASHING TIME. Protestants want simple worship. They destroy Catholic statues of saints, so that people will not honour them, but pray only to God.

HELL FIRE. Mary I (1553–1558) becomes queen. She is a Catholic, and thinks Protestants are wrong. But Protestants won't give up their beliefs, so Mary burns their leaders – alive.

Handy hint

In 16th-century England, you're bound to offend someone by talking about your beliefs. So keep your thoughts to yourself – even holy ones!

BREAKING AWAY. The Catholic Church is led by the Pope in Rome. England's King Henry VIII (1509–1547) quarrels with the Pope for personal reasons. He sets up a new independent Church in England.

BOY REFORMER. Henry's son, Edward VI (1547–1553) becomes king aged nine. He says the new Church in England must be Protestant, and orders a prayer book that everyone must use.

ALL CHANGE – AGAIN! Mary dies, and Elizabeth I (right) is queen. She supports Protestants. In the north of England, Catholics rebel against her.

IN CONTROL!
Elizabeth I (1558–1603) makes new laws. There will be only one Church in England. It will be Protestant. The English king or queen will be its leader.

PEACE – AT A PRICE. Elizabeth says everyone must attend Protestant Church. All other worship is banned. It's peaceful, but there's no religious freedom.

Early years

MOTHER KNOWS BEST.
Fawkes's mother and her family are Recusants, so she teaches him Catholic prayers.

LISTEN AND LEARN.
Fawkes's teacher, a Recusant, passes on Catholic ideas to pupils.

NEW FATHER, NEW FAITH.
Fawkes's stepfather Bainbridge helps him study the Catholic faith.

HUSH HUSH! Recusants worship at home, with lookouts at the door. They don't want their unlawful prayer-meetings to be discovered.

Want to worship your own way?

Most English people obey Queen Elizabeth's laws. But hundreds – maybe thousands – do not. They simply won't go to a Protestant church. Instead, they worship in the old Catholic way – privately, in secret. They are called 'Recusants': it means 'people who refuse'. Your master, Dennis Bainbridge, is a Recusant. So is his wife Edith, and his stepson, Guy Fawkes. (And so, of course, are their servants, including you.) Just 20 years old, Guy Fawkes is clever, ambitious and longs for adventure. To you, he's a bit of a hero.

RISKY MISSION. A few English Catholics go to Europe to become monks and nuns, or train as priests. They return, in disguise, to lead Recusant worship.

PRIESTS IN PERIL. Many Recusant houses have 'priest holes' – secret spaces where Catholic priests can hide. If caught, priests face the death penalty. The English government says they are traitors.

CRUEL FATE. In York city centre in 1586, Recusant Margaret Clitherow is executed for hiding Catholic priests. Many fearful Recusants are in the crowd that sees her die.

Should you flee, and seek your fortune?

Big excitement! Guy Fawkes is leaving England. He's decided to go to Europe and find work as a soldier. He'll fight in the armies of Catholic rulers: the kings of France and Spain. He's asked you to go with him, as his servant. Think carefully! It's a risky decision. The pay's good, but a soldier's life is tough, dirty and dangerous. You'll be treated as an enemy of England. Abroad, you'll meet other English Recusants – Fawkes makes friends with soldier Thomas Wintour. You'll also be followed by English government spies!

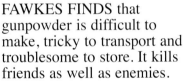

Handy hint

Want to belong to the band of brothers? It helps to learn the local language. When Fawkes joined European armies, he changed his name, from English 'Guy' to Italian 'Guido' (Gwee-doh).

FAWKES FINDS that gunpowder is difficult to make, tricky to transport and troublesome to store. It kills friends as well as enemies.

CONGRATULATIONS! Fawkes wins praise for his expert use of explosives at the siege of Calais, France, in 1596. By 1603 he's been promoted to officer rank.

Hot Stuff!

In the 1590s, gunpowder was the latest high-tech weapon. A mixture of three chemicals, it created massive explosions when set alight. Guy Fawkes learned how to handle gunpowder in Europe, using its deadly power to smash holes in city walls and blow up roads, bridges and large buildings.

Will you welcome the new king?

Meanwhile, back in England, Queen Elizabeth has died. The next king will be her cousin, James VI of Scotland. In 1603, he arrives in London, and is greeted by cheering crowds. King James is a Protestant but his mother, Mary Queen of Scots, was a famous supporter of the Catholic church. Because of this, Recusants like Guy Fawkes hope that James will get rid of the strict laws that limit Catholic worship in England.

GOOD NEWS?
In Spain, Fawkes and Thomas Wintour hear that James VI (known as James I in England) will be their new king.

MARKED MEN.
Fawkes and Wintour return to England in 1604. But English government spies are watching and listening, and follow them.

Hmmm! The English seem quite friendly – so far!

Handy hint

Don't get too excited! King James is a cautious, canny Scotsman. He's not planning to do anything in a hurry.

BIBLE STUDY.
James I has a keen interest in religion. He asks top English Protestant scholars to prepare a new, more accurate, translation of the Bible into English. The 'King James Bible' still survives today, and is praised for its beautiful – if old-fashioned – language.

Henry VII
of England (C)

Henry VIII
(C&P)

Margaret = James V
(C)   of Scotland
(C)

Edward VI
(P)

Mary I
(C)

Elizabeth I
(P)

Mary Queen of Scots
(C)

C = Catholic
P = Protestant

James VI of Scotland/
James I of England
(P)

Can you find friends who share your fears?

You're not just shocked, you're angry! Back in England, you discover that King James won't give Catholics the religious freedom they long for. Even worse, after James hears rumours of a Catholic conspiracy, he announces plans to take legal rights away from even the most peaceful English Catholics. Something must be done! Guy Fawkes and his friends decide to take action. You are with them as they meet at the Duck and Drake Inn in London, and plan the Gunpowder Plot!

WHAT'S THE PLOT? It's simple! (1) Blow up King James. (2) Kidnap his daughter, make her queen, and force her to obey you. (3) Make her change the laws so that Catholics have religious freedom.

18

Who's who? Chief plotters

There have already been several Catholic plots against English Protestant rulers. Now, in 1604, there's a new one – and Guy Fawkes is part of it!

ROBERT CATESBY. A rich country gentleman and fine swordsman, he's the leader. A keen, well-known Recusant, he took part in a failed rebellion against Queen Elizabeth in 1601.

JOHN WRIGHT. He's known Guy Fawkes since they were boys; they went to the same school. He's been in prison after earlier plots and is lucky to have survived.

THOMAS BATES. One of Catesby's servants, he's overheard details of his master's plot. So he's been asked (or made) to join, and sworn to secrecy.

THOMAS WINTOUR. A scholar and a soldier; already a good friend of Guy Fawkes. Together, they're determined to fight for religious freedom.

THOMAS PERCY. Member of an ancient noble family, he has fought (like Guy Fawkes) overseas. The plotters hope that his powerful relatives might help them.

ROBERT WINTOUR and **CHRISTOPHER WRIGHT.** Brothers of two leading plotters, they've already helped Catholic rebels and sheltered Catholic priests.

ROBERT KEYES. A dangerous, desperate man, he's lost all his money and will do almost anything to survive. He's looking after the plotters' secret stores of gunpowder.

JOHN GRANT. A keen supporter of the Catholic cause, his task is to stir up a Catholic rebellion in the English Midlands.

Thomas Bates · *Robert Wintour* · *Christopher Wright* · *John Wright* · *Thomas Percy* · *Guy Fawkes* · *Robert Catesby* · *Thomas Wintour*

Do you really want to kill King James?!

Catesby's Gunpowder Plot is bold – and bloody. Do you think it's a good idea? Once a year, the King visits Parliament to declare its meetings open. The royal family and all the most important people in England go with him. The House of Lords – where the king will make a speech – is at first-floor level, away from the noise, dirt, bustle and smell of the street. There is a dusty cellar underneath. In summer 1604, plotter Thomas Percy rents rooms close by, and Fawkes (disguised as caretaker 'John Johnson') moves in. Now they're ready for the next step....

King

Members of Parliament

Cellar

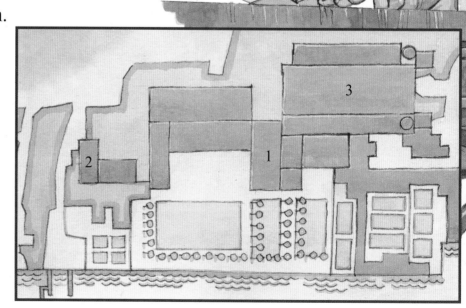

CENTRE OF POWER.
In Guy Fawkes's time, just like today, the English Parliament met in buildings known as the Palace of Westminster. Members debated in the House of Commons (1), the House of Lords (2) and Westminster Hall (3).

Handy hint

Fear 'the Fox' – wily politician Robert Cecil, Earl of Salisbury. He helps run a network of English government spies. How many have you spotted so far in this book?

Is this all TOO easy?

Some historians think that the Gunpowder Plot was encouraged by secret agents working for the English government. Their aim was to trap English Catholics and make them seem wicked and disloyal.

Who will do the dreadful deed?

Prepare for another shock – your master, Guy Fawkes, is given the task of blowing up King James! He's the only plotter with experience of explosives. But even so, this will be mass murder! In secret, the plotters dig a tunnel from Percy's rented rooms to the cellar under the House of Lords. Fawkes goes back to Europe to beg Catholic rulers to support his plans. But – understandably – they are not keen on killing kings. Catholic priests in England are horrified, and try to stop the plot. But everyone ignores them.

The plot progresses...

DODGY DEAL. Only government troops are allowed to have gunpowder. But Fawkes finds ways to get some, from criminals, thieving soldiers – or pirates!

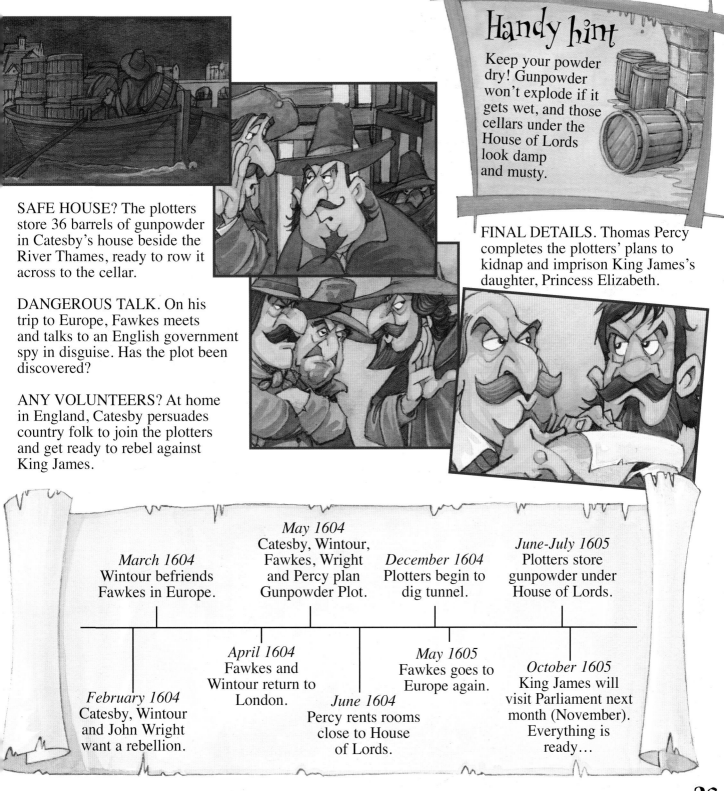

SAFE HOUSE? The plotters store 36 barrels of gunpowder in Catesby's house beside the River Thames, ready to row it across to the cellar.

DANGEROUS TALK. On his trip to Europe, Fawkes meets and talks to an English government spy in disguise. Has the plot been discovered?

ANY VOLUNTEERS? At home in England, Catesby persuades country folk to join the plotters and get ready to rebel against King James.

Handy hint

Keep your powder dry! Gunpowder won't explode if it gets wet, and those cellars under the House of Lords look damp and musty.

FINAL DETAILS. Thomas Percy completes the plotters' plans to kidnap and imprison King James's daughter, Princess Elizabeth.

March 1604 Wintour befriends Fawkes in Europe.

May 1604 Catesby, Wintour, Fawkes, Wright and Percy plan Gunpowder Plot.

December 1604 Plotters begin to dig tunnel.

June-July 1605 Plotters store gunpowder under House of Lords.

February 1604 Catesby, Wintour and John Wright want a rebellion.

April 1604 Fawkes and Wintour return to London.

June 1604 Percy rents rooms close to House of Lords.

May 1605 Fawkes goes to Europe again.

October 1605 King James will visit Parliament next month (November). Everything is ready…

Can you keep the plot a secret?

Yes, you can, and so can Guy Fawkes, your master. But someone has 'spilled the beans'. Today, about a week before the king's scheduled visit to Parliament, a Catholic nobleman, Lord Monteagle, has received an anonymous letter. It warns him to stay away from the House of Lords. Who sent it? Nobody knows. In the past, Monteagle's taken part in Catholic rebellions and paid enormous fines for being a Recusant. But since then, he's promised to be loyal to the king. Whose side is he really on? And what's going to happen now?

OH NO! On 26 October 1605, when Monteagle reads the warning letter, he is horrified – or maybe just pretends to be.

SPREAD THE WORD. Monteagle shows the letter to government minister Robert Cecil, 'the Fox'. Cecil tells King James.

YEARS LATER, after the plot, King James gives Monteagle a rich reward, and poets praise him for saving England.

Handy hint

Don't put anything criminal in writing – even to help your friends. Without Monteagle's warning letter, the Gunpowder Plot might never have been discovered.

INSIDE INFORMATION. A Catholic royal servant warns Catesby that James has suspicions. But Catesby decides to go ahead with the plot!

Who sent the letter?

We really don't know, but the following people have been suggested:

One of the plotters?

Monteagle himself?

A government spy?

A frightened servant?

'Go home to your own county; there, you can wait for the event in safety ... they shall suffer a terrible blow at this Parliament...'

MONTEAGLE'S LETTER aimed to reveal – and stop – the Gunpowder Plot. The sender was either loyal to King James, or frightened of being caught and punished as a plotter.

Will you escape, and survive?

Disaster! Royal bodyguards search Parliament, twice. At midnight on 4th/5th November 1605, they find the cellar full of gunpowder – and arrest Guy Fawkes! He's been hiding there, getting ready for the following morning, when he plans to set off a massive explosion to kill the King. Fawkes is still pretending to be caretaker John Johnson, but the royal guards are suspicious. They say he's a "desperate fellow…up to no good". The other plotters are trying to escape from London. Join them – and run for your life!

Seize the villain!

The plot that stopped!

STEP 1: Guy Fawkes gathers all the things he needs to start the explosion on time, and hides them under his clothes.

Watch

Candle (for flame)

Fuse

Touchwood (kindling)

Handy hint

Hide the evidence! Lurking in the dark with gunpowder is very suspicious, but having fuses, a timer and touchwood makes Fawkes seem doubly guilty.

STEP 2: Fawkes checks the stacks of gunpowder in the cellar under the House of Lords.

STEP 3: Fawkes adds firewood, touchwood and a fuse (rope soaked in a fast-burning chemical).

STEP 4: Fawkes will light the fuse. It will carry a flame to the gunpowder and set it on fire.

STEP 5: Fawkes will flee from the force of the explosion.

STEP 6: Everyone in the House of Lords will be killed by the blast.

Could you survive terrible torture?

Now the news gets worse! You learn that Fawkes has been dragged in front of a frightened but furious King James, then, a few hours later, bullied, beaten, questioned and threatened again. Both times, he has refused to reveal the names of other plotters, or give details of the Gunpowder Plot. So now he's in prison. That's a fate worse than death! You also hear rumours of a shoot-out between escaping plotters and law-officers, in the English Midlands. Some plotters are feared dead. Try to hide!

WE HAVE WAYS of making you talk! King James orders torture, to force Guy Fawkes to tell all he knows.

What would you say?

IF YOU had been caught redhanded, ready to blow up Parliament, how would you explain yourself? Would you:

I want to blow you Scotch beggars back to your Scotch mountains!

Apologise and admit your guilt?

Or be bravely defiant, like Guy Fawkes?

Blame others for the plot?

Guido Fawkes

G.

Say you know absolutely nothing?

Handy hint
Think about it! Guy Fawkes planned to kill, and that was wicked. But he also refused to betray his friends. Was that right or wrong?

FORCED TO CONFESS. Guy Fawkes is taken to the Tower of London. We don't know exactly what happens there, but, five days later, he is broken in body and spirit. His signatures before torture (above) and after (below) show how much he suffered.

...then face a dreadful death?

So now you know. It's bad news. Nine of the plotters have been captured, along with friends who helped them. English Protestants are delighted that the Gunpowder Plot has been stopped; so is King James, of course. He doesn't blame peaceful English Catholics, but he does want revenge on the plotters. In January 1606, they are put on trial. Most beg for mercy, but Fawkes is defiant. Yes, he wanted to kill the king! He's not sorry! The plotters are found guilty. They must die.

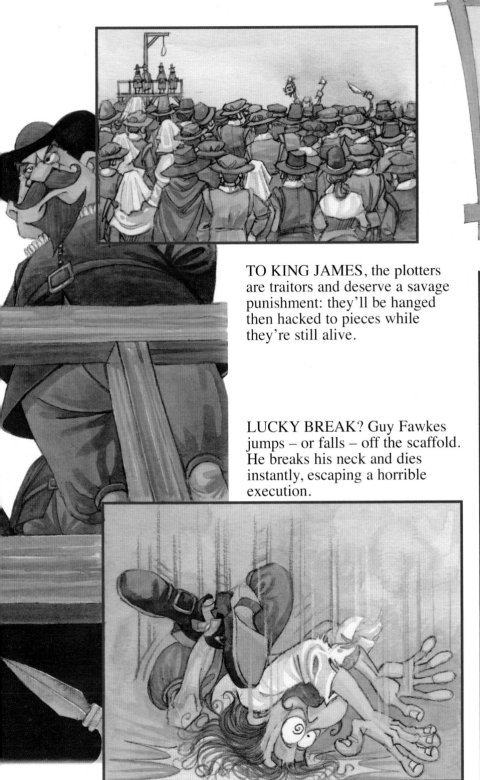

Stay away from the ravens! They live in the Tower of London, and feast on the flesh of criminals who have been executed.

TO KING JAMES, the plotters are traitors and deserve a savage punishment: they'll be hanged then hacked to pieces while they're still alive.

LUCKY BREAK? Guy Fawkes jumps – or falls – off the scaffold. He breaks his neck and dies instantly, escaping a horrible execution.

No escape!

WHAT HAPPENS TO THE PLOTTERS, AND FRIENDS?

ROBERT CATESBY, Thomas Percy, John Wright and Christopher Wright die in a gun fight with government law officers.

ROBERT AND THOMAS WINTOUR, Thomas Bates, Robert Keyes, Ambrose Rookwood, John Grant and Sir Everard Digby are cruelly executed. Bits of their bodies are displayed on the Tower of London's walls.

FRANCIS TRESHAM dies in prison, probably from poison.

FATHER HENRY GARNET, senior Catholic priest in England, is executed, even though he has tried to stop the Gunpowder Plot.

Will they remember, remember...?

Phew! You've had a lucky escape! You stowed away on a French ship moored in the River Thames, and now you're safe in Europe. But you hear that England's Parliament has given orders for 5th November to be a 'joyful day' – forever. English Protestants celebrate by holding special church services, ringing church bells and lighting bonfires. These fires are often topped by a life-size effigy (model figure) of the Pope. If you could travel forward in time, you'd see that many people still hold 'Bonfire Night' parties today. But the figure they burn is dressed as Guy Fawkes. What a tragic way to be remembered!

GOD SAVE THE KING!

"Remember, remember The 5th of November, Gunpowder, treason and plot!

We know no reason Why gunpowder treason Should ever be forgot..."

THE GUNPOWDER PLOT was a failure, but it was never forgotten. This rhyme was first written down around 1870, but it is hundreds of years older.

EVER SINCE 1606, Yeoman Warders (royal bodyguards) have searched Parliament buildings every year on 5th November, in memory of the Gunpowder Plot.

TODAY, parliaments in many lands face deadly new threats from terrorists. In London, Parliament buildings are protected by armed guards and huge blocks of concrete.

Handy hint

Find out more about bonfires! Using a library or the internet, what can you discover about bonfires and fireworks, all around the world?

33

Glossary

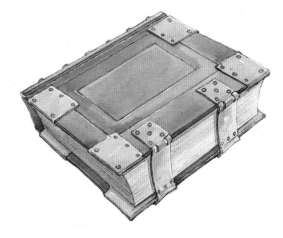

Canny Clever, cautious, sensible.

Catholic Church A branch of the Christian Church headed by the Pope in Rome, Italy.

Catholics Men, women and children who belong to the Catholic Church, share its beliefs and worship in the way it teaches.

Conspiracy A secret plan to do something that is harmful or against the law.

Defiant Refusing to do what you should do, or what someone orders you to do.

Effigy A model figure of a man or woman, often life-size.

Execution Killing as a punishment.

Gunpowder The first high-explosive to be invented (around AD 900, in China). It was used in European wars after around 1400. It is a mixture of three chemicals blended together.

Moored (used to describe boats). Tied to a fixed point, such as a harbour wall.

Pope The head of the Catholic Church, based in Rome, Italy. Catholics believe that the Pope has special authority, given to him by God, to rule the Catholic Church and guide Catholic believers.

Priest hole A secret space in a building where Catholic priests hid.

Protestants Men and women who disagree with some religious teachings of the Catholic Church. In the past, they also criticised the way some Catholic priests behaved, and the way the Catholic Church was run. From the 16th century onwards, groups of Protestants in Europe and America broke away from the Catholic Church and set up new, independent, reformed Protestant churches of their own.

Recusants People who refuse to obey. Guy Fawkes and many other English Catholics were Recusants. In England, there were also small groups of Protestant Recusants who refused to obey Queen Elizabeth's religious laws.

Reform To improve, re-organise, and change things that are wrong.

Scaffold A tall platform, usually made of wood. In the past, used for executions.

Touchwood Little pieces of dried, rotten wood that catch fire very easily.

Yeomen Warders Royal bodyguards, based at the Tower of London. Today, they are sometimes called 'Beefeaters'.

Index

B
Bates, Thomas 19, 31
bonfires 32, 33

C
Catesby, Robert, 19, 20, 23, 25,
  31
Catholic
  priests 10, 13, 19, 22, 31
  rebellion 11, 19, 23, 24
  rulers 10, 11, 17, 22
  worship 10, 12, 13, 16
Cecil, Robert (the 'Fox') 21, 24
chief plotters 19
Christian religion 10
Clitherow, Margaret 13
confession 29

D
death penalty 13
Duck and Drake Inn 18

E
effigy 32
English government 13, 21
Europe 10, 13, 14, 15, 22, 23

F
fines 13, 24
fireworks 33
France 14, 15

G
government spies 14, 16, 21, 23,
  25
gunpowder 15, 19, 22, 23, 27

H
House of Commons 20
House of Lords 20, 22, 23, 24,
  27

K
King Edward VI 11
King Henry VIII 11
King James I 16, 17, 18, 23,
  24, 25, 28, 31
King James Bible 17

L
Latin 10

M
Monteagle's letter 24–25

P
Parliament 20, 32
Percy, Thomas 19, 20, 23, 31
Pope 11, 32
priest holes 13
Protestant
  preachers 10
  rulers 16, 19
  scholars 17
  worship 10, 11
punishment 13, 28–29, 31

Q
Queen Elizabeth I 11
Queen Mary I 10

R
ravens 31
Recusants 12, 13, 19
religion 10–11, 12–13, 16, 17,
  18
religious reform 10, 11
'Remember, remember' rhyme
  32

S
Siege of Calais 15
Spain 14, 16

T
torture 28–29
Tower of London 29, 31
tunnel 22, 23

W
Westminster Hall 20
Wintour, Robert 19, 31
Wintour, Thomas 14, 16, 19, 23,
  31
Wright, Christopher 19, 31
Wright, John 19, 23, 31

Y
Yeoman Warders 32
York 9

Guy Fawkes, hero or villain?

Guy Fawkes and his fellow plotters had strong and sincere beliefs. Yet they planned to kill and injure many innocent people because they disagreed with them about religion. This was wrong.

At the same time, the King and Parliament in England used fines, threats and extreme violence to stop people like Guy Fawkes worshipping in the way they wanted to. This was also wrong.

Guy Fawkes was brave and daring, but he was not a hero. Nor was he a complete villain. Instead, he was a victim of his own troubled times. Have we learned from his story? Very sadly, no. People today still fight and kill because of religious disagreements.

Readers, as you think about Guy Fawkes, please also think about this: however strong and sincere your beliefs, and whatever your religion, please do not ever use violence to settle your quarrels with governments or with other people.

Bonfires and fireworks

Bonfires were originally 'bone-fires' – heaps of animal bones burned by early farmers, after they had killed sheep and cattle for food. Fire was the best way to dispose of smelly, bloody old bones; the flames killed dangerous germs from the dead animals.

In many lands, people used to light bonfires to celebrate the changing seasons. Autumn and winter fires imitated (copied) the heat and light of sun and encouraged it to return; spring and summer fires drove out cold winter and welcomed back the warm, bright, strengthening sun.

Bonfires were also said to bring new life. In Scandinavia, and in ancient Rome, young couples leaped across the flames; they hoped this would keep them healthy and give them many children. In Japan, bonfires were lit to welcome back the ghosts of dead ancestors.

Fireworks were invented in China over 1000 years ago. Their loud noise was meant to keep dangerous spirits away, but they soon became part of festivals and celebrations. They were made from gunpowder (another Chinese invention) packed into a hollow bamboo tube.

The first firework displays in Europe took place in the 1400s. Italian inventors mixed chemicals with gunpowder to create coloured patterns in the sky. Early fireworks exploded in brilliant flashes of white, orange and yellow, but by the 20th century, chemists had discovered how to create fireworks in red, blue, green, silver and gold.

Today's fireworks are extreme! A firework rocket roars into the air at 150 miles per hour and soars 200 metres above the ground. A little hand-held sparkler can reach a temperature of up to 1500°C.

Hi guys!

Guy Fawkes's life – and death – gave a new word to the English language. At first, after 1606, a 'guy' was a life-sized effigy (model figure) dressed in old clothes, burnt on a bonfire (see pages 32-33). From around 1850, the word guy was used to describe a rough, ragged or dangerous-looking man. By the 20th century, especially in America, 'guy' simply meant 'a male person'. It was often used by people who wanted to sound modern and fashionable, or casual and relaxed. Today, the word's meaning has changed yet again. We now use phrases such as 'hi guys' and 'you guys' when speaking to groups of male and female friends.

Good Guys, bad Guys

When Guy Fawkes was born, his parents chose to give him an ancient name that was fairly well known throughout Europe. But after the Gunpowder Plot, mothers and fathers in England were afraid to use it for their children, in case people thought that they supported Fawkes's murderous plans. Recently, the name Guy has become more popular; there were 67 babies called Guy in England and Wales in 2014, out of a total of 356,772 newborn boys.